Rotten kids are welcome!
Munchkins come along.
Bring your ankle-biter friends.
Yard apes, too, belong.

Hooligans, punks and
Tattletales and brats.
Come and join the
with the stinkers and

Laughing Gas

Rotten Rhymes & Scraps of Hot Air

Poems By Michele Glassford
Illustrations by Lisa Lach

Dedicated to Keah, Paolo & rotten kids everywhere!

WARNING: Readers who have forgotten how to laugh and have fun exit stage left.

Printed in Canada

ISBN 0-9781559-0-4

PRO3 18 10 06

Library and Archives Canada Cataloguing in Publication

Glassford, Michele
Laughing gas : rotten rhymes and scraps of hot air / Michele Glassford ; illustrator, Lisa Lach.

ISBN 0-9781559-0-4

1. Children's poetry, Canadian (English). 2. Humorous poetry, Canadian (English). I. Lach, Lisa II. Title.

PS8613.L385L38 2006 jC811'.6 C2006-904955-6

Table of Contents

Lisa Lach

"In the game of poker, a Royal Flush conists of an Ace, King, Queen, Jack and ten all of the same suit. It is the highest possible hand in poker."

Buckingham Palace in London, England, home to Queen Elizabeth II, has 78 bathrooms.

I can still hear my mother's judicious advice,
"Very few squares from the roll should suffice.
If you use any more, I'm sure that you know,
You'll cause a momentous commode overflow."

Well, I didn't listen – my mom's always wrong.
I reeled off a strip more than three miles long.
Into the toilet it went, then I flushed,
And watched as the water rose quickly, then gushed.

It went over the seat and onto the floor,
Swirled past the bathtub and under the door,
To the top of the stairs at the end of the hall,
Where it cascaded down in a huge waterfall.

It seemed I had made a most dreadful mistake.
I peered in the kitchen and discovered a lake.
I knew I must stop it, I knew I must try,
When I spotted my sister go dog-paddling by.

I went back through the murgling, gurgling slop,
I lunged for the plunger and reached for the mop.
I plunged and I mopped 'till I could mop no more.
My brow was perspiring, my fingers were sore.

I guess I learned something while cleaning that mess.
Why I didn't listen is anyone's guess.
The lesson I learned, now I'll share it with you –
Why use three miles when just one mile will do?

Naked As A Jaybird

Going Commando!

While swimming once when it was hot,
My underwear I had forgot.
Not being one to scream and shout,
I decided just to go without.
Though not as bad as I had feared
The feel of it was really weird.
The breeze blew up into my shorts
And whispered to my nether parts.
I felt as free and light as air,
Unburdened by my underwear.
Though feeling shame a bit, I'd bet
Now every time I might forget.

I'm naked as a
jaybird,
I haven't a stitch on.
I dove into the water,
Surprise! My suit
was gone.
I'm naked as a
jaybird,
And that's not really
fair.
'Cause jaybird has
his feathers,
And what I have is
bare.

Wedgie War

My brother's always planning.
He likes the sneak attack,
And when I am not looking,
Pulls my undies up my back.
Although he knows I hate it,
It's his best weapon of choice.
It leaves me in discomfort,
With a high and squeaky voice.
Revenge is swift and painful.
While brother slept in bed,
I grabbed and pulled his undies,
All the way over his head.

LOVE HANDLES

I hate my name! It's really gross,
And I can only blame my folks.
I'd be content, I do believe
If I could be a Nick or Steve.
I'm sure it would remove my shame,
If they would only change my name.
But my parents could be really vicious
And change me to an Aloysius.
So I stick with who I am, of course,
And will remain a Wilberforce

The top ten baby names for girls and boys in 2005 were: Emma, Emily, Madison, Kaitlyn, Sophia, Isabella, Olivia, Hannah, Makayla, Ava, Aidan, Jacob, Ethan, Nicholas, Matthew, Ryan, Tyler, Jack, Joshua, Andrew

In 1910: Mary, Helen, Margaret, Dorothy, Ruth, Anna, Mildred, Elizabeth, Alice, Ethel, John, William, James, Robert, Joseph, Charles, George, Edward, Frank, Henry.

www.everything2.com reports that the longest recorded name is Adolph Blaine Charles David Earl Frederick Gerald Hubert Irvim John Kenneth Loyd Martin Nero Oliver Paul Quincy Randolph Sherman Thomas Uncas Victor Willian Xerxes Yancy Zeus wolfeschlegelsteinhausenbergerdorffvoralternwarengewissenhafschafersweschafewarenwholgepflegeundsorgfaltigkeitbeschutzenvonangereifenduchihrraubgiriigfeindewelchevorralternzwolftausendjahresvorandieerscheinenbandererssteerdeemmeshedrraumschiffgebrauchlichtalsseinursprungvonkraftgestartseinlangefahrthinzwischensternartigraumaufdersuchenachdiesternwelshegehabtbewohnbarplanetenkreisedrehensichundwohinderneurassevanverstandigmenshlichkeittkonntevortpflanzenundsicherfreunanlebenslamdlichfreudeunruhemitnichteinfurchtvorangreifenvonandererintlligentgeschopfsvonhinzwischensternartigraum, Senior.

Apparently the name was shortened to Mr. Hubert Wolfe, though officially it was said that he signed his name Hubert Blaine Wolfeschlegelsteinhausenbergerdorff, Sr.

froggy weather

there's a frog on my head.
don't ask me why.
it's just where it landed,
when it fell from the sky.
now it's hitching a ride
on the top of my bean.
it's the most absurd thing
that i've ever seen.
now my long journey
has gone to the dogs.
cause i had no umbrella
when it rained
hats & frogs.

As recently as June 2005, it was reported that it rained thousands of frogs on Odzaci, Serbia, Belgrade when a small tornado picked up the frogs over a pond and dumped them on the town.

Limbo is a competitive dance, originating in Trinidad and Tobago. How low can you go?

herbie the worm

herbie the worm has no
hands and no feet,
but he dreams of becoming
a star athlete.
when others tell him that
he cannot compete,
he tells them they're wrong
and that he won't be beat.
explaining that high jump
is now obsolete,
herbie cleans up at the
limbo dance meet.

sweet!

BUBBLES

Bathtub bubbles just won't stop

Backyard bubbles fun to pop.

The opposite of a bubble is an antibubble which is a drop of water surrounded by a thin skin of air. A water droplet is an antibubble, as is a water droplet which "floats" either in or on another body of water.

Bubbles in my soda -- SLURP!

Bubbles in my belly

BUUURRRPPP!!!

Excuse Me!

I Feel Fowl

Like every kid around my block,
I'm haunted by the kitchen clock.
For every tick and every tock
Brings yet another chicken pock.

The itchiness you cannot match,
It's like a poison ivy patch.
My fingers ready to dispatch,
But wait -
I'm not supposed to scratch!

I cannot scratch, I cannot rub,
I sit in oatmeal in the tub.
I wish I'd had the chance to snub
This calamine pink lotion club.

I'm speckled with all
kinds of spots.
My face is freckled with red dots,
They're in my ears and
through my thoughts,
I'm covered with red blobs and
blots.

I can't go out
with friends to play,
Inside the house I'm told to stay,
And it has only been one day!
Oh, will they ever, ever,
ever,
ever,
ever,
ever go away?

Buffet

Cow patties,
Prairie chips,
Moose muffins,
Sheep dip,
Road apples, elk duds,
Rabbit raisins and kitty buds,
Lawn sausage, leopard loaf,
Buffalo bagels, enough, enough!
All these thoughts have left me queasy –
Feeling rather baddish.
And I'll never, ever, ever, ever, ever eat horseradish.

In A Pickle

In a pickle,
In a mess,
In a quandry,
I confess,
Up the creek,
Without a doubt,
I'm in trouble.

Get me out!

This saying dates back to the 1600s. The word "peckel" is a Dutch word for brine. So, to be "in a pickle" was to be in a strong, sour mess.

Cleaning Bites!

I told my Mom I'd clean my room.
She handed me a boring broom.
The mere thought filled me up with doom,
So I went and got the new vacuum.

I plugged it in and held my breath.
The dust bunnies faced certain death,
And all the dirt would soon be gone.
I closed my eyes and switched it on.

It jumped to life with hum and roar.
I started cleaning up my floor.
I reached under my bed and "SSSLUP!"
It sucked my precious kitty up.

I gasped and looked into the hose.
It started to suck up my nose.
I pulled away and pushed it back,
To try to stave off its attack.

It grabbed my socks right off my feet
And ate them like a candy treat.
For life I clung to my toy bin,
To keep from getting sucked right in.

Its humming put me in a trance
As it took hold and ate my pants.
All I could do was stop and stare
As I stood there in my underwear.

I shook my head to stay alert.
It caught the corner of my shirt.
I tugged and pulled to keep it out
But still my shirt went up the spout.

I turned and ran toward my door,
I couldn't stay one second more.
I knew it in my heart and soul,
If I stayed I would be eaten whole.

But wait! It's only a machine,
To help you keep your carpets clean.
So I faced it with a mighty tug,
And managed to pull out the plug.

The room was now quite calm and still.
I sat and gathered up my will.
I thought I'd take it from the top.
"Hey Mom, can you get me the mop?"

APPENDAGES

Where can I put my arms when I get into bed?
Should I fold them on my chest, or put them on my head?
I could keep them by my sides, but then I cannot roll.
I need to find some comfort.
It's my only goal.
But my arms are in the way.
And I'm sick of counting sheep.
If I could only take them off, then I could get some sleep.

Excuuuuuse me!

Farts and fluffers,
Ponks and puffers,
Break an ill wind,
Drop a bomb,
Raise a stink,
Pass some gas,
But try to do it with
some class.

Some people fart after they are dead!

Crack one, rip one,
Cut the cheese,
But always say, "Excuse me, please."

Farts are composed mostly of nitrogen and carbon dioxide, but some may also contain hydrogen, oxygen and methane.

An average person farts around 14 times a day [about a half litre of gas per day.]

Poop Happens

Listen up, now here's the scoop.
It turns out life is full of poop.
So keep your steps within your sight,
If you want to keep your sneakers white.

Scratch & Sniff
Just Kidding!

Pull My Finger

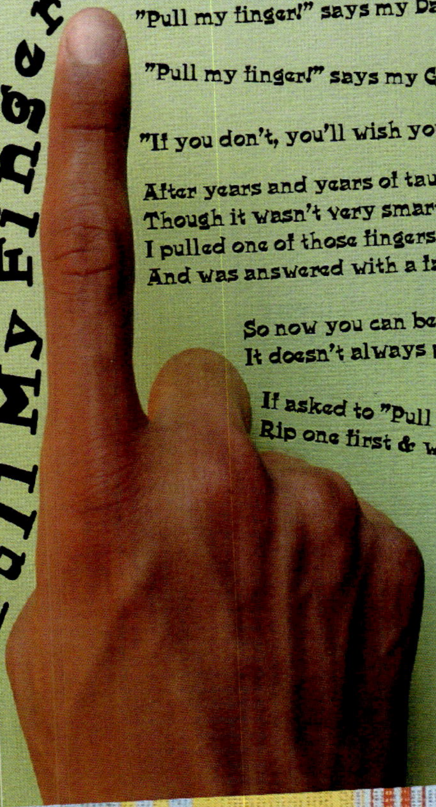

"Pull my finger!" says my brother.
"Pull my finger!" says my Dad.

"Pull my finger!" says my Grandpa,

"If you don't, you'll wish you had!"

After years and years of taunting,
Though it wasn't very smart,
I pulled one of those fingers
And was answered with a fart!

So now you can believe me.
It doesn't always pay.

If asked to "Pull my finger"
Rip one first & walk away!

Foods such as cauliflower, eggs and meat
make stinkier farts than beans
because they have more sulphur content.

Whoever Smelled It...

Who's to blame?
It's usually me,
When a stink rises up
accusingly.
It wasn't me.
I really swear.
No warm spots on my underwear.
When we emerge,
Out from the fog,
Mom blames me, I blame the
dog.

Termites are the fartiest animals on earth.

Don't Toot in Your Snowsuit

Please heed this warning!
Please take my advice!
I know from experience –
At least once or twice.

Whatever you do–
If you have to toot,
Do not ever do it
Inside your snowsuit.

A snowsuit covers from
Your neck to your toes.
And bad hot air rises
Straight up to your nose.

If my hair was cold SPAGHETTI, with green OLIVES for my eyes
And my lips were long red PEPPERS, I'd be sure to realize,
That my ears are really CAULIFLOWERS, and my skin is PIZZA DOUGH
My nose is made of MEATBALL, and it's really hard to blow.
My eyebrows would be smoked SARDINES, TOMATOES for my cheeks.
My face would be the most DELICIOUS meal I've had in weeks.

PEAS

I admit that I like spinach
And the lowly lima bean,
The acorn, the zucchini
And all squashes in between.
Brussel sprouts and broccoli,
And turnips, if you please.
But I really, really, really, really
Really hate green peas.

I don't know why I hate them.
There's no reason, I suppose.
They even come in perfect size
For sticking up your nose.

But I refuse to eat them.
End of dialogue.
I hide them underneath my plate
Then feed them to the dog.

Will Beg For Food

Achoo!

When I sneeze
I have no grace.
I find I can't
control my face.
When I sneeze,
please give me space.
I always spray
all over the place.

The speed of a sneeze
can be 150 km/h or
almost 100 mph

ICK

Don't pick or flick the ick that you
find inside your nose.
Don't stick into your mouth or lick
the gick between your toes.
They're habits to kick,
'Cause you'll make yourself sick
And better stuff's in your ears,
don't you knows?

SICK

My stomach aches,
My head is sore,
I know I cannot take much
more.

My skin has bumps,
My eyeballs itch,
My neck's developing a
twitch.

My knees they knock,
I have a tic,
I must be terribly, terribly
sick.

The doctor checks.
My fear dispels.
I'm sick with worry -
nothing else.

Most animals sneeze, however, iguanas are the animals known to sneeze the most.

LICK

Every single thing I saw
I felt I had to lick.
My mother told me not to,
Said it would make me sick.

I felt compelled to use my tongue,
To discover taste and feel.
I really couldn't help myself,
Didn't see what's the big deal.

But when the winter came about,
I just ran out of luck.
I licked the metal flagpole,
My tongue got truly stuck.

Now I will remember,
For avoiding further harm,
My tongue must stay inside my mouth,
At least until it's warm.

Your tongue will stick to metal at -5C. So don't even think about trying it!!

FACE FREEZE

Grandma said my face will freeze,
If I pull an ugly mug.
"You expect me to believe that?"
I answered with a shrug.
But then I looked around and saw
A face unlike another.
Though reluctant to believe my gran,
It might explain my brother.

The Thniffles

No one wanth to be awound be.
'Cauth I weally god 'em bad.
Eberyone gibs be tithues.
It'th the wortht I'be eber had.
I honk, I thnort, I gurgle, too.
When I'm drying do bweathe.
You thee I'be god duh thniffles.
Wadch oud! I'm going to thneethe!

Best Friend

I hate my best friend and she hates me.
We annoy each other constantly.
We tease and fight and never share.
I poke at her. She pulls my hair.
We want to play at different games.
We call each other nasty names.
She makes me really, really mad.
She's the bestest friend I've ever had.

Dirty Laundry

My favorite pairs of
underwear,
Of which you may be
unaware,
Though not entirely
unique,
Are named for each day
of the week.

Not under bed, nor on the
floor,
I keep them neatly in my
drawer,
Ironed, folded, put away,
Until I wear each on its
day.

Then Monday, when I did
the wash,
The machine it rumbled,
churned and sloshed.
Though six went in, without
a doubt,
Just five pairs managed to
come out.

The morning after, just
past dawn,
I woke to find my
Tuesday gone,
And though it filled me
up with dread,
I put on Wednesday's
pair instead.

Then Thursday became
Friday
Or was it Wednesday still?
Maybe now it's Saturday.
I cannot really tell.
I think that it's the weekend,
unless I am a fool,
and staying home on Monday
when I should be in school.

I'm overly dependent on my
undies,
I confess.
And now that one is missing,
My life's a total mess.
I do not know what time it is,
I'm starting to despair.
But I guess that now the time
has come
to get new underwear.

SECRET

I must tell you a secret.
I know you'll be discreet.
I was born with suction cups,
Instead of hands and feet.

I'm really not embarrassed,
'Cause no one really cares,
Until they see me climbing walls
Instead of taking stairs.

The Collector

Recently, a collection of 1500 Silverage comic books sold for over $4,000 US. What do you collect - toe jam, belly button fluff or eye boogers? JUST KIDDING!!

A box of snails, some bottle caps, and extra special rocks,
Some candy wrappers, bouncy balls, and multi-coloured socks,
Weirdly-shaped erasers, and pencils with designs,
Tiny bits of sea glass and sea shells of every kind,
Stickers and the little books you need to stick them in,
Dozens of the fake tattoos for slicking on my skin.
Now I sit admiring my excellent selection
'Cause I know I have the very best collection of collections.

Did you know corkscrew collectors are known as helixophiles?

A person who collects postage stamps is called a philotelic, a person who collects coins is a numismatic, a person who collects books is a bibliophile.

Hey Diddle Dreaming

Sometimes when it's late at night,
And all the stars are shining bright,
Through my window I calmly stare,
And imagine taking flight.

Despite my rocket's fiery glare,
I would not go just anywhere,
But maybe Saturn or Neptune
Or Pluto if I dare.

As I pass beside the moon,
Travelling in my tin cocoon,
I wish I may, I wish I might,
See the cow and dish and spoon.

"Hey, Diddle, Diddle" is a traditional English folk song first published in 1765.

UNDER THE BED

Under the bed hide monsters and such
Hideous things that I'd rather not touch.
Slobbery things with six eyes and two heads,
Even worse than the ones under other kids' beds.

I haven't the courage to look under yet,
It's crowded with fears that I'd rather forget.
I'm feeling too frightened, I'm feeling too weak
But maybe I will....
just take one little peek.

With one eye wide open, the other shut tight
I peered underneath through the cavernous light.
And sitting right there,.... waiting to pounce...,
Was my lost basketball which still had some bounce.

There were five or six socks, but none made a pair,
Nestled beside some old underwear.
Some puzzles and toys, a new baseball bat,
Old homework that must have been chewed by the cat.

**UNDER THE BED ARE NO MONSTERS I SEE,
JUST A MONSTER-SIZED MESS, LEFT THERE BY ME!**

Redecorate

Green gives me comfort.
Pink makes me sleep.
Red makes me angry.
Grey makes me weep.
Yellow makes me happy.
White gives me hope.
Purple gives me courage.
Black makes me mope.
Brown's warm and fuzzy.
Blue makes me sad.
What colour will I
paint my room?
I think I'll paint it plaid.

Researchers at the Children's Emergency Center of Udine, Italy, found that children sleeping less than 10 hours a day is associated with an 86% increase in injury risk.

Zonked

I'm getting really punchy.
My wheels are falling off.
I'm bagged,
I'm dragged,
I'm spent,
I'm whacked,
But I refuse to hit the sack.
I'm tired beyond reason.
I'm totally played out.
I'm pooped,
I'm bushed,
I'm zonked,
I'm dead,
But I will not,
WILL NOT go to bed.
Alarm clock keeps on ringing
As Mom calls from the stairs.
I trying hard
To be inspired.
I can't get up, I'm just
too tired.

Credits and Acknowledgments

Title Page- Bazzill Basics Paper, Wishblade
page 5- Bazzill Basics Paper www.greenpeace.ca, June 2006, www.britainexpress.com, June 2006
page 6- Bazzill Basics Paper
page 7- Bazzill Basics Paper, www.everything2.com, June 06, baby names from www.babycentral.com, June 06
page 8- Basic Grey "Jackson", Bazzill Basics Paper, www.allaboutfrogs.org, June 2006
page 9- Bazzill Basics Paper, Basic Grey "Jackson", www.antibubble.org, June 2006
page 10- Basic Grey "Cherry Pie", Bazzill Basics Paper, Wishblade
page 11- Basic Grey "Mesmerize", Bazzill Basics Paper, www.word-detective.com 021402, June 2006
page 12- Bazzill Basics Paper, Mary Bellis "The History of Vacuum Cleaners" http: inventors.about.com, June 06
Page 14- Basic Grey "Believe", Bazzill Basics Paper, Facts on Farts Brenna Lorenz www.heptune.com, June 06
Page 15- Basic Grey "Believe", Facts on Farts by Brenna Lorenz www.heptune.com, June 2006
Page 17- Bazzill Basics Paper
Page 18- Basic Grey "Jack Frost" "Dasher" "Holly", Bazzill Basics Paper, Pressed Petals Scrap Metal, menshealth.about.com, James Fussell, "Your Sneeze Trumpets the Inner You", The Seattle Times, January 4, 06.
Page 19- Basic Grey "Jack Frost" "Dasher" "Ribbon Candy" "Holly", Bazzill Basics Paper, Pressed Petals
Page 20- Basic Grey "Taylor" "Madison", Bazzill Basics Paper
Page 21- Bazzill Basics Paper
Page 22- Basic Grey "Velvet Stocking", Bazzill Basics Paper, Wishblade
Page 23- Bazzill Basics Paper,
Page 24- Basic Grey "Hydro" "Lulu" "Slo Mo", Bazzill Basics Paper, www.rhymes.org.uk, June 2006
Page 25- Basic Grey "Strawberry Jam", Bazzill Basics Paper, www.sleepfoundation.com, June 2006
Page 26- Basic Grey "Believe"
Page 27- Basic Grey "Believe"
Page 28- Basic Grey "Verona", Bazzill Basics Paper, handmade Tear Bears
Back Cover Bazzill Basics Paper

Special thanks to Susan Zambiasi, Amy Romano, Nick Curtis of nickcurtisfonts.com for permission to use his fonts, Wishblade (wishblade.com), Pressed Petals Inc., BasicGrey, LLC (basicgrey.com), Bazzill Basics Paper (bazzillbasics.com), Casper the friendly dog, and of course, all of our families and friends for their support.

www.laughinggaspress.com

Warning: Gas is no laughing matter

Use the space below to write your own rotten rhyme

Michele Glassford

A wise person once told me that you should try to make a living doing what you loved to do as a kid. Since there was no way to make a living picking my nose and playing in mud, I decided to try my hand at my third favourite childhood pastime - rotten rhymes. And since growing up and becoming a Mom I find there's no shortage of rotten kids doing rotten things to inspire me.

Lisa Lach

An apple may be rotten, but it's not rotten to the core. Isn't that true for the rotten kid in all of us? As a single Mom, Writer, Illustrator and Scrapbook Queen, there aren't enough pages in the world to cover all the crazy moments in my life's journey. But I keep trying! So let me scrap yours.

www.scrapnthat.com